● Smithsonian

Exploring

the

Pennsylvania
Colony

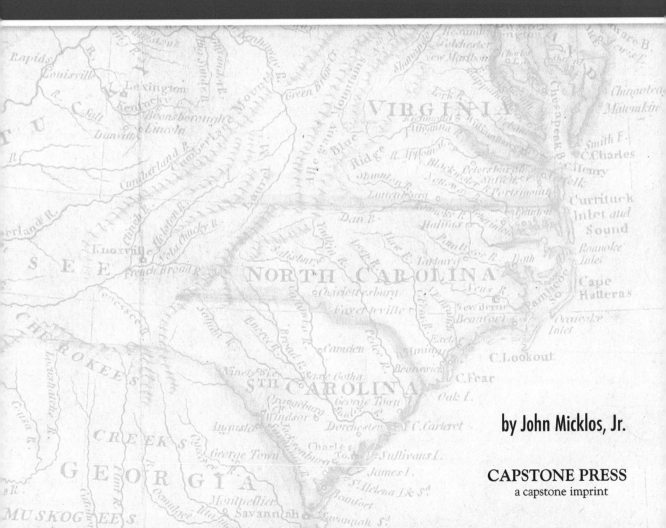

by John Micklos, Jr.

CAPSTONE PRESS
a capstone imprint

Smithsonian Books are published by Capstone Press,
1710 Roe Crest Drive, North Mankato, Minnesota 56003
www.capstonepub.com

Library of Congress Cataloging-in-Publication Data
Names: Micklos, John, author.
Title: Exploring the Pennsylvania Colony / by John Micklos, Jr.
Description: North Mankato, Minnesota: Capstone Press, [2017] | Series:
  Smithsonian. Exploring the 13 colonies | Includes bibliographical
  references and index. | Audience: Ages 8-11.
Identifiers: LCCN 2016008181| ISBN 9781515722328 (library binding: alk.
  paper) | ISBN 9781515722458 (pbk.: alk. paper) | ISBN 9781515722588
  (ebook: .pdf)
Subjects: LCSH: Pennsylvania—History—Colonial period, ca.
  1600–1775—Juvenile literature. |
  Pennsylvania—History—1775–1865—Juvenile literature.
Classification: LCC F152 .M595 2017 | DDC 974.8/02—dc23
LC record available at http://lccn.loc.gov/2016008181

Editorial Credits
Gina Kammer, editor; Richard Parker, designer; Eric Gohl, media researcher;
Kathy McColley, production specialist

Our very special thanks to Stephen Binns at the Smithsonian Center for Learning and Digital Access for
his curatorial review. Capstone would also like to thank Kealy Gordon, Smithsonian Institution Product
Development Manager, and the following at Smithsonian Enterprises: Christopher A. Liedel, President;
Carol LeBlanc, Senior Vice President; Brigid Ferraro, Vice President; Ellen Nanney, Licensing Manager.

Photo Credits
American Philosophical Society: 19; Bridgeman Images: Peter Newark American Pictures/Private
Collection, 25; Capstone: 4, 21; Corbis: Bettmann, 27; Getty Images: Curt Teich Postcard Archives, 13;
Granger, NYC: 6, 22, 40; Library of Congress: 32, 33, 35; Nativestock: Marilyn Angel Wynn, 8; North
Wind Picture Archives: cover, 7, 9, 10, 11, 12, 14, 16, 17, 18, 20, 23, 24, 26, 28, 29, 30, 31, 34, 36, 38, 39, 41;
Wikimedia: Public Domain, 15, 37

Design Elements: Shutterstock

Table of Contents

PENNSYLVANIA

Introduction:
The 13 Colonies

Creating the 13 Colonies

Virginia, the first permanent English **colony** in America, was settled in 1607. Pennsylvania was nearly the last of the original 13 Colonies that became the United States. Swedes first settled Pennsylvania in 1643, but it wasn't officially **chartered** by the English until 1681. Only Georgia was founded later—in 1733. The colonies stretched along the coastline of the Atlantic for roughly 1,500 miles. They extended from Georgia to what is now the state of Maine.

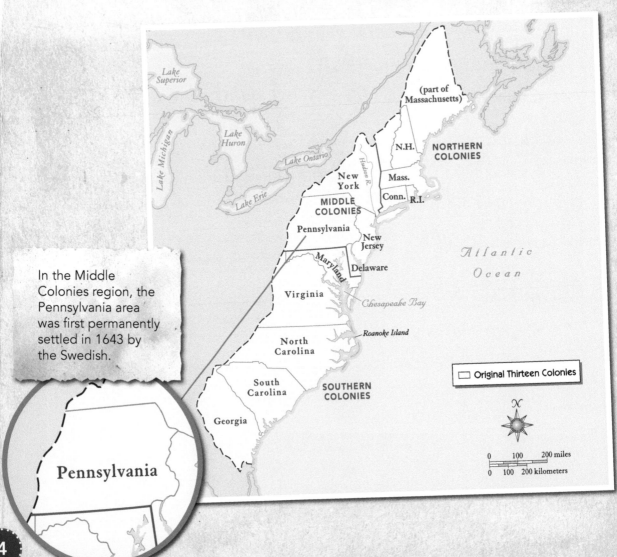

In the Middle Colonies region, the Pennsylvania area was first permanently settled in 1643 by the Swedish.

The Original 13 Colonies

The first permanent European settlement in each colony:

Virginia	1607	Delaware	1638
Massachusetts	1620	Pennsylvania	1643
New Hampshire	1623	North Carolina	1653
New York	1624	New Jersey	1660
Connecticut	1633	South Carolina	1670
Maryland	1634	Georgia	1733
Rhode Island	1636		

Colonies are areas controlled by another country. Generally the country that controls the colony is far away. Early settlers of the 13 Colonies came for a variety of reasons. Some came in search of religious freedom. Others simply sought a better way of life in a new land.

In the 1600s Sweden, the Netherlands, and England all established colonies along the eastern coast of what is now the United States. By the late 1600s, England controlled all of these colonies. Each colony had its own government. However, England ruled them all from across the Atlantic Ocean. England hoped to benefit from the rich **natural resources** in this new land.

colony—a place that is settled by people from another country and is controlled by that country

charter—an official document granting permission to set up a new colony, organization, or company

natural resource—a material found in nature that is useful to people

The land and climate of Pennsylvania were good for growing crops, such as corn and wheat.

PENNSYLVANIA

Pennsylvania's support of religious freedom drew many **immigrants** from Europe. It attracted people from other colonies as well.

Settlers were also attracted by the **fertile** farmland and long growing season of this colony. Two key crops were corn and wheat. Pennsylvania's central location among the colonies allowed it to easily export goods to other colonies. Philadelphia became an important port city and grew rapidly.

By the 1760s the colonies had complaints against England. They did not like the taxes that England placed on them. By the 1770s some colonists were discussing breaking away from England. They wanted to form an independent nation.

Because of its central location, Pennsylvania became the gathering place for Colonial political meetings. Philadelphia was the capital of the 13 Colonies for most of the American Revolution. The Declaration of Independence and the U.S. Constitution were signed there. From its humble beginnings, Pennsylvania became one of the most important colonies.

Philadelphia quickly grew into an important city. Its location made it a good place to do business.

immigrant—someone who settles permanently in another country
fertile—good for growing crops; fertile soil has many nutrients

Chapter 1:
Pennsylvania's Native Americans

PENNSYLVANIA

As in other colonies, early settlers in Pennsylvania found well-established Native American societies. Tribes such as the Lenni Lenapes (also called the Delawares), Shawnees, Nanticokes, and Mingos had roamed the forests and fields for centuries. In fact, **artifacts** suggest that Native Americans first arrived in Pennsylvania 10,000 to 12,000 years ago. Most of these tribes lived by farming, hunting, and fishing.

Life in a Native American Village

The Lenni Lenapes lived in simple one-family houses made of bark set on poles. For food they relied on corn, beans, and squash. They called these foods the "Three Sisters." They also ate meat, sweet potatoes, nuts, and fruits. Women did the cooking. Men hunted deer and bears for both food and clothing. They trapped beavers and traded the furs with white settlers. Young boys learned to hunt and work with wood. Girls learned to cook, garden, and keep house. For clothing men wore animal skins or a cloth around their waists and moccasins. Women wore knee-length skirts.

Lenni Lenape people used a stone and grinding rock, such as this one, to make flour from corn.

Europeans Arrive

The first contact between Europeans and Native Americans in Pennsylvania probably occurred in 1608 or 1609. English colonist John Smith sailed north to the region from Virginia in 1608. Englishman Henry Hudson, sailing for the Dutch, explored the area in 1609.

By 1638 Swedish and Dutch settlers began forming settlements along the Delaware River in what is now southeastern Pennsylvania. Most of these settlements remained small, and relations between the Europeans and the Native American tribes were mostly friendly. William Penn, the English founder of the colony, arrived in 1682. He quickly met with chiefs of the Lenni Lenape tribe. Penn called for the settlers and Native Americans to live together in peace.

A chief named Tamanend is believed to have said: "We will live in love with William Penn and his children as long as the creeks and rivers run, and while the sun, moon, and stars endure." There is no written record of a peace treaty made between Penn and Tamanend. According to legend the record was woven into a **wampum belt**, which was later lost.

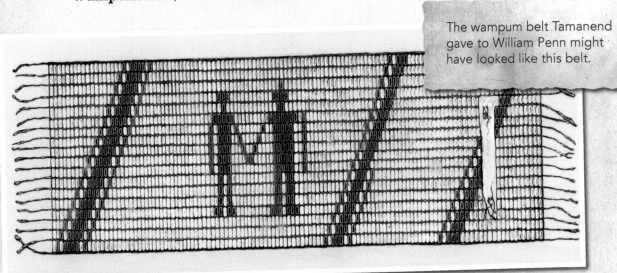

The wampum belt Tamanend gave to William Penn might have looked like this belt.

artifact—an object used in the past that was made by people
wampum belt—a belt with shell beads (wampum) used for gifts or for recording stories

Relations with the native tribes remained friendly for many years. This changed after Penn died. In 1737 Penn's sons cheated the Lenni Lenapes out of a huge area of land. Penn's son Thomas claimed to have a deed that said the Penns could have as much land as a man could walk in a day and a half from a certain starting point. The Penns hired three trained runners, who covered an amazing 66 miles. Chief Nutimus said, "If this practice must hold, why then we are no more Brothers and Friends but much more like Open Enemies." Soon the Native Americans were forced to move away.

The colonists lost their friendship with the Lenni Lenapes after trained runners claimed much of the Lenni Lenape land in 1737.

George Washington attacked the French forces in the French and Indian War to defend England's colonies.

Going to War

Both France and England wanted to control land in North America. This led to the French and Indian War (1754–1763) in North America. Many tribes sided with the French. They fought against British troops and the colonists. They hoped to keep more settlers from moving onto their land. Other tribes sided with the British and colonists. They feared they would lose their trading partners if the colonists left.

During the French and Indian War, Native Americans launched many raids on Pennsylvania's western frontier. A young **militia** officer named George Washington fought in several battles against the French and Native Americans. He distinguished himself as a brave leader. The war finally ended with the total defeat of the French. The British gained most of France's land in North America, which included New France (present-day Canada).

militia—a group of citizens who are organized to fight, but who are not professional soldiers

Soon the British and the colonists claimed even more tribal land. As a result the Native American warrior Pontiac, of the Ottawa tribe, led attacks on forts and settlements. From 1763 to 1766, Pontiac's War raged from the Great Lakes to Virginia. Several battles occurred along the Pennsylvania frontier. In December 1763 a militia group called the Paxton Rangers killed 20 peaceful members of the Conestoga tribe living near Lancaster, Pennsylvania. Many people were outraged by these murders. The governor of Pennsylvania—William Penn's grandson John Penn—called for the killers to be brought to justice. That never happened.

A treaty signed in 1766 ended Pontiac's War. Settlers moved further west and north across Pennsylvania. Soon nearly all of the Native Americans had been forced out. Many others had died of disease over the years. Europeans had brought diseases such as **smallpox** and measles to America. Native Americans had no **immunity** to these diseases. Some Native American villages were nearly wiped out.

Chief Pontiac led Native Americans in attacks against the colonists.

Teedyuscung (1700–1763)

One Delaware chief named Teedyuscung tried to bring peace during the French and Indian War. He claimed to be "King of the Delawares." He offered to convince the Native Americans to stop fighting against the British and colonists. In return he wanted the colonists to promise to protect his tribe's land. At a treaty meeting in 1757, he asked for "a certain Country fixed for our own Use, and the Use of our Children forever." But his efforts failed because the colonists wanted that rich land. Teedyuscung was murdered in 1763 when someone set fire to his cabin while he slept. His dreams of peace were never fulfilled.

smallpox—a disease that spreads easily from person to person, causing chills, fever, and pimples that scar

immunity—the ability of the body to resist a disease

Chapter 2:
A New Type of Colony

The first European settlers arrived in the region now known as Pennsylvania in 1638. Led by Peter Minuit, Swedish settlers built a trading post named Fort Christina along the Delaware River in present-day Wilmington, Delaware. They called the area New Sweden. In 1643 they moved their capital a few miles north. It sat just a few miles south of where Philadelphia is today.

Swedish colonists arrived and settled along the Delaware River in 1638.

The Swedish colony did not last long. In 1655 Dutch soldiers arrived from their colony of New Netherland to the north. Some Swedes left. Others swore their loyalty and support to the Dutch. The Dutch colony did not last long either. In 1664 the British captured New Netherland and renamed it New York. The Dutch land further south was renamed New Jersey. The land west of the Delaware River (what is now Pennsylvania) remained mostly unsettled.

Critical Thinking with Primary Sources

New Sweden existed as a colony for just a few years. However, the Swedes were the first to build log cabins in the area. This log cabin still exists in present-day Pennsylvania. Why do you think log cabins made sense for colonists' homes? What do you notice about how the logs were stacked? How do you think colonists sealed their cabins?

William Penn Forms a Colony

The colony of Pennsylvania came about because King Charles II of England owed a large debt to Admiral William Penn. When the admiral died, the king had not yet paid the debt. The admiral's son, also named William Penn, had an idea. He asked the king to repay the debt by giving him land in America. There he would start a new colony based on the idea of religious freedom.

The king granted Penn 45,000 square miles in 1681. The land stretched west from the Delaware River. Penn arrived from England in October 1682 to see his new property. One of his first acts was to meet with leaders of the Lenni Lenape tribe. The Great Treaty they agreed upon promised peace. Penn wanted to name the land New Wales, because its rolling hills reminded him of the hilly country of Wales. The king decided to name it Pennsylvania, in honor of Penn's father.

Quakers worshipped freely in the Pennsylvania Colony.

PENNSYLVANIA

William Penn (1644–1718)

The son of a wealthy British admiral, Pennsylvania's founder belonged to the Society of Friends (or Quakers). This religious group believed all people were equal in the eyes of God. Its members refused to swear loyalty to the king. As a result Quakers were treated poorly in England. Penn himself was jailed several times because of his beliefs. He wanted to start a colony that allowed religious freedom. He called his colony a "holy experiment." However, Penn had to put much of his wealth into building and growing the colony. He lost his fortune and died penniless in England.

Penn immediately began building the city of Philadelphia. The city's name means "brotherly love" in Greek. Penn wanted his new city and colony to reflect that openness and love. Pennsylvania became known for offering religious freedom. Many Quakers came, and some assumed leadership roles. People from many other religions came too.

Did You Know?

The name Pennsylvania means "Penn's woods."

17

PENNSYLVANIA

Penn served as governor of the colony. However, he wanted others to have a voice too. He set up a form of government that allowed fairly wide representation among the colony's voting citizens. This did not include everyone. Women couldn't vote. Neither could slaves nor **indentured servants**.

In 1701 Penn approved a new constitution, called the Charter of Privileges, which gave voters greater control over the government. This constitution remained in place until the American Revolution, 75 years later.

William Penn's constitution allowed for changes, just like the U.S. Constitution, which was written nearly a century later.

> *"no Person . . . shall be . . . compelled to frequent or maintain any religious Worship, Place or Ministry, contrary to his or their Mind . . ."*
>
> —William Penn from his Charter of Privileges, 1701

Pennsylvania thrived. But Penn had borrowed huge sums of money. He returned to England in 1701 but couldn't pay his debts. In 1708 he was placed in debtor's prison for a year. His health declined, and he never returned to Pennsylvania. His wife and sons took control of the colony. They governed it until 1775.

Critical Thinking with Primary Sources

William Penn's Charter of Privileges set guidelines for governing the colony. Among other things, it guaranteed religious freedom to the people of Pennsylvania. Why was religious freedom so important to the Quakers? How was that different from the practices of some other colonies?

indentured servant—a person who works for someone else for a certain period of time in return for payment of travel and living costs

Chapter 3:
Growth and Expansion

Philadelphia quickly grew into a successful city. Located where the Schuylkill and Delaware Rivers meet, it became a key trading and shipbuilding center. Wheat, corn, and other crops from the rich farmland nearby came into the city. From there crops were shipped to the other colonies. In fact Pennsylvania became known as a "breadbasket" colony because of all the food it produced. Its location near the geographic center of the colonies helped. The colony also shipped goods to Europe.

Industries and Businesses Develop

A mill industry soon developed throughout the Pennsylvania Colony. Sawmills sprang up along many streams. These mills turned raw timber into boards for building houses. **Gristmills** ground grain into flour. Across the colony blacksmiths hammered iron into horseshoes and other useful goods. As Philadelphia grew colonists set up all sorts of businesses. For example, inventor and businessman Benjamin Franklin established a newspaper. He later published the popular *Poor Richard's Almanack*. This short book, published yearly, was full of poems, wise sayings, and information on the weather.

Benjamin Franklin worked in the printing business and published newspapers and books.

> *"Lost time is never found again."*
>
> *"No gains without pains."*
>
> *"Well done is better than well said."*
>
> —Ben Franklin's sayings from *Poor Richard's Almanack*

Settlers Spread Out

As the colony's population continued to increase, other cities began to develop. These included Lancaster, Bethlehem, York, and Reading.

Immigrants flocked to Pennsylvania from across Europe. Many came from Germany. In the early 1700s, many German-speaking Amish people began to settle in the Lancaster area. They remain a strong influence today. The Amish believe in living simply and dressing plainly. Even today they travel by horse and buggy, and use limited forms of electricity in their homes. They are known as expert farmers, bakers, and woodworkers.

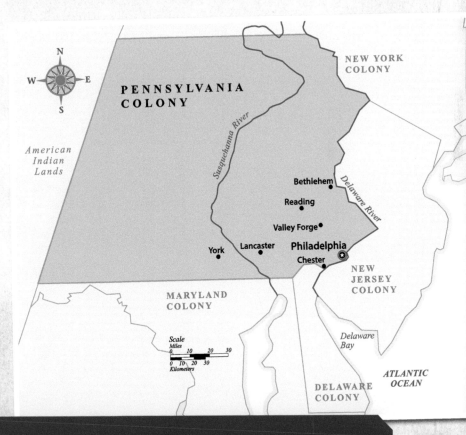

gristmill—a mill that grinds grain into flour

PENNSYLVANIA

Over time Pennsylvania's settlers moved further north and west. They expanded into the Lehigh Valley and Pocono Mountains. They reached the Pittsburgh area in the 1750s. Still, settlement of the central and western sections of the colony remained slow until the late 1700s.

By the end of the Colonial period in 1776, Pennsylvania was the third most populous colony after Virginia and Massachusetts. Philadelphia had a population of roughly 30,000. It ranked as the second-largest English-speaking city in the world. Only London had more people.

Did You Know?

For years Pennsylvania argued about its borders with neighboring colonies Maryland and Delaware. In the 1760s Charles Mason and Jeremiah Dixon examined the area to resolve the dispute. They set a boundary known as the Mason–Dixon Line between Pennsylvania, Maryland, and Delaware. During the Civil War, the Mason–Dixon Line became the informal border between the North and South.

Benjamin Franklin (1706–1790)

Scientist. Inventor. Author. Printer. Politician. Diplomat. Benjamin Franklin was all of these things and more during his long life. At age 17 he ran away from his family in Boston and traveled to Philadelphia. Soon he had established a successful printing business. He also helped the city succeed. He formed America's first subscription library, organized Philadelphia's first fire company, and helped launch a hospital.

Franklin was also a gifted inventor. His many inventions included bifocals, the lightning rod, and the Franklin stove, all of which are still used today. He gained his greatest fame for his experiments in electricity.

During the Revolutionary War (1775–1783), Franklin helped draft the Declaration of Independence and served as an **ambassador** to France. Later he signed the U.S. Constitution and became president of an antislavery society. He ranked among the most famous and admired people of the 1700s.

ambassador—a person sent by a government to represent it in another country

Chapter 4

Daily Life in Colonial Pennsylvania

PENNSYLVANIA

Daily life in Colonial Pennsylvania depended on where people lived and how much money they had. City life differed from country life. And the lives of rich people differed greatly from those of working-class or poor people.

City Life and Work

In the cities people made a living in different ways. Many young boys became **apprentices**. This meant that they worked with a skilled craftsman to learn a trade. Key trades included shipbuilding, blacksmithing, printing, and shoemaking. Some people ran clothing, food, or medicine shops. Few women held jobs outside the home. Those who did often worked as **seamstresses**, shopkeepers, nurses, or **midwives**.

A master woodworker would teach his apprentice about the woodworking trade.

There were few slaves in Pennsylvania. But there were thousands of indentured servants. In exchange for passage to America, these servants agreed to work for a certain number of years. Then they were free to go out and get a job. Sometimes they had learned a trade along the way.

Life in the Country

Families in the country lived mostly off the land. They raised chickens and cows for eggs and milk. They made their own bread and ate fruits and vegetables that they grew. They hunted wild game for meat. Everyone worked hard from dawn to dusk. Many families even made their own clothes.

Did You Know?

The first paper mill in North America was built in 1690 near the Germantown section of Philadelphia.

Pennsylvania families in the country farmed the land for their own food and to trade.

apprentice—a person who works for another to learn a trade or craft
seamstress—a woman who sews for a living
midwife—a person who helps women in childbirth

Childhood in Colonial Pennsylvania

Most Colonial families had many children. This made sure there were lots of hands to share the work. Also many children died young from diseases such as measles or smallpox.

Colonial children led hard lives. They had many chores. On farms they gathered eggs, milked cows, and helped tend crops. In cities they did chores around the house.

In Colonial times few children received a formal education. Public schools were rare. The children of wealthy families often learned at home from private tutors. Yet Colonial Pennsylvania was a leader in education. Many Quaker communities provided basic education to young children. The first elementary school in Philadelphia opened in 1689. The school reflected William Penn's spirit of equality. Children from wealthy families paid a fee and poor children were taught for free.

Children in the Pennsylvania Colony often learned to read and write in one-room schoolhouses.

Colonial children played a game called "hoops."

In their leisure time, children played outside. Young girls had simple dolls made of wood or rags. Boys would use wooden sticks as pretend horses or guns. Children sometimes made spinning tops out of wood and string. They jumped rope and played leapfrog, tag, or hide-and-seek. They also played "hoops," a game in which they rolled a barrel hoop with a stick.

Focus on Religion

For most Quaker families, life centered on their faith. Quakers gathered in meetinghouses. Quaker services took different forms. Some services were highly unstructured. People entered and sat together in silence. The goal was to open one's mind in what was often called "expectant waiting." People spoke when they believed they had a message to share.

Quakers gathered in meetinghouses such as this one in Philadelphia.

Did You Know?

Nearly half of the immigrants coming to America during Colonial times came as indentured servants.

Daniel Boone (1734–1820)

Born in eastern Pennsylvania in 1734, Daniel Boone became a famous **trailblazer**. He grew up in the woods and was said to have killed his first bear while still a youngster.

As an adult, although happily married with 10 children, Boone loved adventure and exploring. During one of his trips, he found a gap through the Appalachian Mountains. In 1775 he led settlers through this gap to an unsettled area in Kentucky. He named the settlement Boonesborough. Over the years Boone survived several run-ins with unfriendly Native Americans, and his legend grew. It's hard to know where the facts end and the legend begins. But one thing is certain. Daniel Boone was one of Colonial America's top **frontiersmen**.

trailblazer—a person who makes new trails through unexplored areas
frontiersman—a person who is skilled at living outside settled land

Chapter 5:
A Center of Independence

PENNSYLVANIA

During the 1760s the British taxed the colonies to help pay the costs of the French and Indian War. The colonists thought these taxes were unfair because the colonies were not represented in Parliament, Britain's lawmaking body. In 1766 Benjamin Franklin stood before the British House of Commons to argue against the very unpopular Stamp Act. The act required that a tax stamp be placed on most paper goods, such as newspapers. Franklin's arguments helped bring an end to the tax.

Protests and Penalties

The most famous tax protest took place in Boston in December 1773. Colonists dressed as Native Americans threw British tea into the harbor. Following this incident, known as the Boston Tea Party, Britain passed laws to punish the residents of Massachusetts. Among other things these laws—which the colonists referred to as the Intolerable Acts—closed Boston Harbor. This cut off all overseas trade. The other colonies, including Pennsylvania, sent food and supplies. But it was clear that further action was needed. A meeting of the colonies was called. Because of its central location, Colonial leaders selected Philadelphia as the meeting place for the First Continental Congress.

In protest against British taxes, American colonists in Boston dumped tea into the harbor.

> *"An internal tax is forced from the people without their consent if not laid by their own representatives."*
>
> —Benjamin Franklin before the House of Commons in London, 1766

Delegates from 12 of the 13 Colonies met for a month in the fall of 1774. (Georgia did not participate.) They voted to **boycott** all British goods if the Intolerable Acts were not **repealed**. The delegates were not yet ready to separate from Britain, but they also didn't feel that Britain had the right to tax the colonies. They sent King George III a list of complaints and a statement of their rights to "life, liberty, and property."

However, Britain refused to change its stance, and relations went from bad to worse. The colonists realized that to gain the freedoms they wanted, they would have to go to war to get it. In April 1775 British troops clashed with Colonial militia in Massachusetts. The Revolutionary War had begun.

In May delegates of the colonies met again in Philadelphia. Although America was already at war with Great Britain, the Second Continental Congress made one final attempt to try to make peace. But it was too late—the king completely refused to receive their request for peace. At the same time, delegates voted to establish a Continental army. They chose George Washington to lead it.

The First Continental Congress in Philadelphia opened with a prayer.

delegate—someone who represents other people at a meeting
boycott—to refuse to take part in something as a way of making a protest
repeal—to officially cancel something, such as a law

Declaring Independence

After King George III rejected the colonies' final request for peace, Colonial leaders debated what to do next. Some still hoped to find a peaceful solution. Others thought the colonies should break away from England and form their own country. In January 1776 Philadelphia resident Thomas Paine published a pamphlet called *Common Sense*. In it he listed reasons why the colonies should declare their independence from Britain. For example, Paine argued, "Europe, and not England, is the parent country of America." He explained that the "new world" had been a shelter for those seeking "civil and religious liberty from *every part* of Europe." However, Paine believed that the colonists still didn't have these freedoms under England's rule. The colonists would need to break with England for the same reasons they had first left their home countries for America.

PENNSYLVANIA

Did You Know?

Thomas Paine's *Common Sense* sold 500,000 copies. This is an amazing number since the entire population of all 13 Colonies at the time was around 2.5 million.

Thomas Paine supported America's freedom from Britain and urged the colonies to declare independence.

> *"Why is it that we hesitate? From Britain we can expect nothing but ruin."*
>
> —Thomas Paine from *Common Sense*, 1776

Critical Thinking with Primary Sources

Thomas Paine's *Common Sense* helped push the colonies toward independence. Why do you think *Common Sense* was so widely distributed and discussed? If the pamphlet had not been written, do you think the colonies still would have declared independence from England?

COMMON SENSE;

ADDRESSED TO THE

INHABITANTS

OF

AMERICA,

On the following interesting

SUBJECTS.

I. Of the Origin and Design of Government in general, with concise Remarks on the English Constitution.

II. Of Monarchy and Hereditary Succession.

III. Thoughts on the present State of American Affairs.

IV. Of the present Ability of America, with some miscellaneous Reflections.

Man knows no Master save creating HEAVEN, Or those whom choice and common good ordain.

THOMSON.

PHILADELPHIA;

Printed, and Sold, by R. BELL, in Third-Street.

MDCCLXXVI.

Thousands of people throughout the colonies read and discussed *Common Sense*. More and more began to believe that the colonies should break away from Britain. The Second Continental Congress discussed whether to take the major step of declaring independence. In the end they decided to formally break free from Great Britain.

PENNSYLVANIA

In this picture, the artist depicted Benjamin Franklin listening to Thomas Jefferson reading the rough draft of the Declaration of Independence.

Congress appointed a committee of five men to draft such a document. Thomas Jefferson wrote most of it, and Philadelphia's Benjamin Franklin helped. On July 4, 1776, Congress adopted the Declaration of Independence. It set forth the reasons for breaking away from Britain. Among other things, the declaration noted that all men should be entitled to "Life, Liberty and the pursuit of Happiness." Now there was no turning back.

Betsy Ross
(1752–1836)

According to legend Betsy Ross designed and sewed the first American flag. Did she really? Most historians think not. We do know she was a seamstress in Philadelphia during the Revolutionary War. We also know that she sewed some of the Continental army's early flags. Did she sew the first American flag or create the design? We'll probably never know for sure. Either way she played an important role in the war effort.

Chapter 6:
Choosing a Capital for a New Country

PENNSYLVANIA

The Declaration of Independence was signed in Philadelphia, and Congress chose the city as a meeting place. With Philadelphia's central location, it made sense that the capital of the new government would reside there. Meanwhile, Pennsylvania made the transition from colony to state. A new state government was established with a new legislature. For the first time since its founding, the Penn family no longer controlled Pennsylvania.

The Second Continental Congress met at Independence Hall in Philadelphia.

Critical Thinking with Primary Sources

The Declaration of Independence is a document that announced that the colonies were breaking away from England. It declared that they would form the United States of America. Why do you think the rights described in the declaration were not extended to women or African-Americans? If the document were being drafted today, what concerns might be addressed that were not concerns at the time?

Rough Beginning, Victorious End

The new national capital got off to a rough start. The Revolutionary War continued, and the British Army swept into Philadelphia in September 1777, occupying the city until June 1778. George Washington tried to stop them from crossing Brandywine Creek south of Philadelphia. However, **Loyalist** farmers led the British Army across at another spot. Hearing confusing reports, Washington wasn't prepared. The Continental army was also less organized, and the British fought fiercely. Washington was eventually defeated.

While the British Army moved into Philadelphia, most **Patriots** moved to the country. Officers moved into the best houses and lived well over the winter. However, George Washington had ordered the removal of any of the city's supplies that the British might use. Washington attacked again on October 4 in the Battle of Germantown, but his army wasn't trained well enough to succeed. They were forced to retreat.

Americans tried to stop the British in the Battle of Brandywine before they could move into Philadelphia.

The new U.S. government also fled on September 30. Its leaders set up operations in York, a city about 100 miles west of Philadelphia. Throughout the war the government also met at various other locations. General Washington's army, meanwhile, spent the miserable winter of 1777–1778 camped at Valley Forge, Pennsylvania. The soldiers often went without food in freezing weather. Despite the terrible weather and lack of supplies, the troops trained and drilled. When spring came they were ready to face the British.

The Continental army struggled through a hard winter at Valley Forge.

Loyalist—a colonist who was loyal to Great Britain during the Revolutionary War

Patriot—a person who sided with the colonies during the Revolutionary War

Meanwhile, Benjamin Franklin continued to play a key role. He traveled to France and convinced the French to support the U.S. war effort. That support helped turn the tide. When the Treaty of Paris was signed in September 1783, the United States had truly gained its independence.

PENNSYLVANIA

This unfinished painting shows the Americans who discussed a treaty with Britain. It includes Benjamin Franklin in the center, wearing black.

"The Keystone State"

The Second Continental Congress met in Pennsylvania for all but a few months of the war. In 1787 Philadelphia hosted the convention at which delegates created the U.S. Constitution. That document established the form of government we still have today. In 1790 after all 13 states had **ratified** the Constitution, the government once again settled in Philadelphia. There it stayed until 1800, when it moved to Washington, D.C.

From humble beginnings, Pennsylvania became one of the most important colonies. It played a key role in the forming of a new nation. Because of that, it truly earned its nickname: "The Keystone State."

The Constitutional Convention was held in Philadelphia in 1787.

Did You Know?

Pennsylvania is one of four states to call itself a **commonwealth**. The others are Kentucky, Massachusetts, and Virginia.

ratify—to formally approve
commonwealth—a region that is governed by the people who live there

Timeline

PENNSYLVANIA

1608–1609   Europeans first make contact with Native Americans in Pennsylvania.

1643 Swedish explorers establish Pennsylvania's first permanent settlement as part of New Sweden.

1655 The Dutch take control of the Swedish territory and name it New Netherland.

1664 The English take control of New Netherland from the Dutch and rename it New York.

1681 William Penn receives a charter for the colony of Pennsylvania.

1682 William Penn visits his new colony and establishes relations with the Native Americans living there. Philadelphia is founded in October.

1701 William Penn presents the Pennsylvania Charter of Privileges, a constitution that guarantees religious freedom "forever."

1731 Benjamin Franklin opens the first subscription library in America.

1737 William Penn's sons cheat the Native Americans out of a large amount of land.

1754–1763   The French and Indian War is fought between Britain and France.

1767 The boundary between Maryland, Delaware, and Pennsylvania is established and is called the Mason–Dixon Line.

1774 The First Continental Congress meets in Philadelphia.

1775 The Revolutionary War begins; the Second Continental Congress meets in Philadelphia.

1776 The Declaration of Independence is signed in Philadelphia, and the city becomes the capital of the new United States.

1777 British troops occupy Philadelphia; Congress moves to York, Pennsylvania.

1778 British troops withdraw from Philadelphia.

1783 The Revolutionary War ends; the United States is recognized as an independent country.

1787 Delegates draft the U.S. Constitution in Philadelphia.

1790 The U.S. Constitution is ratified, making Pennsylvania the second state in the Union. Philadelphia once again serves as the U.S. capital.

1800 The U.S. capital is moved to Washington, D.C.

Regions of the 13 Colonies		
Northern Colonies	**Middle Colonies**	**Southern Colonies**
Connecticut, Massachusetts, New Hampshire, Rhode Island	Delaware, New Jersey, New York, Pennsylvania	Georgia, Maryland, North Carolina, South Carolina, Virginia
land more suitable for hunting than farming; trees cut down for lumber; trapped wild animals for their meat and fur; fished in rivers, lakes, and ocean	the "Breadbasket" colonies—rich farmland, perfect for growing wheat, corn, rye, and other grains	soil better for growing tobacco, rice, and indigo; crops grown on huge farms called plantations; landowners depended heavily on servants and slaves to work in the fields

Glossary

PENNSYLVANIA

ambassador (am-BA-suh-duhr)—a person sent by a government to represent it in another country

apprentice (uh-PREN-tiss)—a person who works for another to learn a trade or craft

artifact (AR-tuh-fakt)—an object used in the past that was made by people

boycott (BOY-kot)—to refuse to take part in something as a way of making a protest

charter (CHAR-tuhr)—an official document granting permission to set up a new colony, organization, or company

colony (KAH-luh-nee)—a place that is settled by people from another country and is controlled by that country

commonwealth (KAH-muhn-welth)—a region that is governed by the people who live there

delegate (DEL-uh-guht)—someone who represents other people at a meeting

fertile (FUHR-tuhl)—good for growing crops; fertile soil has many nutrients

frontiersman (fruhn-TIHRS-muhn)—a person who is skilled at living outside settled land

gristmill (GRIST-mil)—a mill that grinds grain into flour

immigrant (IM-uh-gruhnt)—someone who settles permanently in another country

immunity (i-MYOON-uh-tee)—the ability of the body to resist a disease

indentured servant (in-DEN-churd SUR-vuhnt)—a person who works for someone else for a certain period of time in return for payment of travel and living costs

Loyalist (LOI-uh-list)—a colonist who was loyal to Great Britain during the Revolutionary War

midwife (MID-wife)—a person who helps women in childbirth

militia (muh-LISH-uh)—a group of citizens who are organized to fight, but who are not professional soldiers

natural resource (NACH-ur-uhl REE-sorss)—a material found in nature that is useful to people

Patriot (PAY-tree-uht)—a person who sided with the colonies during the Revolutionary War

ratify (RAT-uh-fye)—to formally approve

repeal (ri-PEEL)—to officially cancel something, such as a law

seamstress (SEEM-struhss)—a woman who sews for a living

smallpox (SMAWL-poks)—a disease that spreads easily from person to person, causing chills, fever, and pimples that scar

trailblazer (TRAYL-blay-zur)—a person who makes new trails through unexplored areas

wampum belt (WAHM-puhm BELT)—a belt with shell beads (wampum) used for gifts or for recording stories

Critical Thinking Using the Common Core

1. What kinds of settlers might have been attracted by Pennsylvania's reputation for supporting religious freedom? How might those people have shaped the colony's development? (Key Ideas and Details)

2. What kind of information in Chapter 6 helps you understand why Philadelphia was such a logical choice to serve as the new nation's first capital? (Craft and Structure)

3. Why do you think Philadelphia became such an important business and intellectual center in the 1700s? (Integration of Knowledge and Ideas)

Read More

Buckley, James, Jr. *Who Was Betsy Ross?* New York: Grosset & Dunlap, 2014.

Figley, Marty Rhodes. *Who Was William Penn? And Other Questions About the Founding of Pennsylvania.* Minneapolis, Minn.: Lerner, 2012.

Rockliff, Mara. *Mesmerized: How Ben Franklin Solved a Mystery that Baffled All of France.* New York: Candlewick Press, 2015.

St. George, Judith. *The Journey of the One and Only Declaration of Independence.* New York: Puffin, 2014.

Internet Sites

FactHound offers a safe, fun way to find Internet sites related to this book. All of the sites on FactHound have been researched by our staff.
Here's all you do:
Visit *www.facthound.com*
Type in this code: 9781515722328

Check out projects, games and lots more at
www.capstonekids.com

Source Notes

PENNSYLVANIA

Page 9, line 14: "William Penn's Treaty with the Indians at Shackamaxon." Penn Treaty Museum. Accessed April 16, 2016. http://www.penntreatymuseum.org/treaty.php.

Page 10, line 8: Steven Craig Harper. *Promised Land: Penn's Holy Experiment, The Walking Purchase, and the Dispossession of Delawares, 1600–1763*. Bethlehem, Pa.: Lehigh University Press, 2006, p. 79.

Page 13, biography box, line 8: Anthony F. C. Wallace. *King of the Delawares: Teedyuscung, 1700–1763*. Philadelphia: University of Pennsylvania Press, 1949, p. 176.

Page 18, callout quote: "Charter of Privileges Granted by William Penn, esq. to the Inhabitants of Pennsylvania and Territories, October 28, 1701." The Avalon Project: Documents in Law, History and Diplomacy. Yale Law School: Lillian Goldman Law Library. Accessed April 16, 2016. http://avalon.law.yale.edu/18th_century/pa07.asp.

Page 21, callout quote: Benjamin Franklin. *Poor Richard's Almanack*. Waterloo, Iowa: U. S. C. Publishing Co., 1914, pp. 35, 39, 57.

Page 31, callout quote: Don Cook. *The Long Fuse: How England Lost the American Colonies, 1760–1785*. New York: The Atlantic Monthly Press, 1995, p. 97.

Page 32, line 8: Thomas Paine. *Common Sense: Addressed to the Inhabitants of America*. Philadelphia: W. & T. Bradford, 1776, p. 65.

Page 33, callout quote: Thomas Paine. *Common Sense: Addressed to the Inhabitants of America*. Philadelphia: W. & T. Bradford, 1776, p. 123.

Page 35, line 6: "Declaration of Independence." *The U.S. National Archives and Records Administration: The Charters of Freedom*. Accessed February 12, 2016. http://www.archives.gov/exhibits/charters/declaration_transcript.html.

Select Bibliography

Brubaker, John H. *Massacre of the Conestogas*. Charleston, S.C.: The History Press, 2010.

Cook, Don. *The Long Fuse: How England Lost the American Colonies, 1760–1785*. New York: The Atlantic Monthly Press, 1995.

"Declaration of Independence." *The U.S. National Archives and Records Administration: The Charters of Freedom*. Accessed February 12, 2016. http://www.archives.gov/exhibits/charters/declaration_transcript.html.

Franklin, Benjamin. *Poor Richard's Almanack*. Waterloo, Iowa: U. S. C. Publishing Co., 1914.

Geiter, Mary K. *William Penn*. London: Pearson, 2000.

Harper, Steven Craig. *Promised Land: Penn's Holy Experiment, The Walking Purchase, and the Dispossession of Delawares, 1600–1763*. Bethlehem, Pa.: Lehigh University Press, 2006.

Isaacson, Walter. *Benjamin Franklin: An American Life*. New York: Simon & Schuster, 2004.

Kelley, Joseph J. *Pennsylvania, the Colonial Years 1681–1776*. Garden City, New York: Doubleday, 1980.

Middleton, Richard. *Pontiac's War: Its Causes, Course, and Consequences*. New York: Routledge, 2007.

Paine, Thomas. *Common Sense*, Edited by Edward Larkin. Peterborough, Ontario: Broadview Editions, 2004.

"The Indians of Pennsylvania." ExplorePAhistory.com. Accessed April 16, 2016. http://explorepahistory.com/story.php?storyId=1-9-14.

"Walking Purchase Historical Marker." ExplorePAhistory.com. Accessed April 16, 2016. http://explorepahistory.com/hmarker.php?markerId=1-A-216.

Wallace, Anthony F. C. *King of the Delawares: Teedyuscung, 1700–1763*. Philadelphia: University of Pennsylvania Press, 1949.

Wallace, Paul A. W. *Indians in Pennsylvania*. Harrisburg: Pennsylvania Historical and Museum Commission, 1961.

"William Penn, Charter of Privileges for the Province of Pennsylvania, 1701." *American Philosophical Society: Treasures of the APS*. Accessed April 19, 2016. https://amphilsoc.org/exhibits/treasures/charter.htm.

"William Penn's Treaty with the Indians at Shackamaxon." Penn Treaty Museum. Accessed April 16, 2016. http://www.penntreatymuseum.org/treaty.php.

Index

PENNSYLVANIA